Pebble Books are published by Capstone Press,
151 Good Counsel Drive, P.O. Box 669, Mankato, Minnesota 56002.
www.capstonepress.com

072011
006231CGVMI

Library of Congress Cataloging-in-Publication Data
Braun, Eric, 1971–
    Tomie dePaola / by Eric Braun.
    p. cm.—(First biographies)
    ISBN-13: 978-0-7368-3641-8 (hardcover)
    ISBN-10: 0-7368-3641-1 (hardcover)
    ISBN-13: 978-0-7368-5093-3 (softcover pbk.)
    ISBN-10: 0-7368-5093-7 (softcover pbk.)
    1. De Paola, Tomie—Juvenile literature. 2. Authors, American—20th century—
Biography—Juvenile literature. 3. Illustrators—United States—Biography—Juvenile
literature. 4. Children's stories—Authorship—Juvenile literature. I. Title. II. First
biographies (Mankato, Minn.)
PS3554.E1147Z58 2005
813'.54—dc22   2004013483

Summary: Simple text and photographs present the life of Tomie dePaola.

Note to Parents and Teachers

The First Biographies set supports national history standards for units on people and culture. This book describes and illustrates the life of Tomie dePaola. The images support early readers in understanding the text. The repetition of words and phrases helps early readers learn new words. This book also introduces early readers to subject-specific vocabulary words, which are defined in the Glossary section. Early readers may need assistance to read some words and to use the Table of Contents, Glossary, Read More, Internet Sites, and Index sections of the book.

Table of Contents

Early Years 5

First Jobs 11

Tomie's Books 13

Glossary 22

Read More 23

Internet Sites 23

Index 24

Time Line

1934
born

Early Years

Tomie dePaola was born in Connecticut in 1934. Tomie's mother read to him. When Tomie was 4, he knew he wanted to write and draw.

Tomie's hometown, Meriden, Connecticut, in 1934

Time Line

1934
born

1952
goes to
art school

Tomie drew lots of pictures as he grew up. He graduated from high school in 1952. He went to art school in New York.

Pratt Art Institute in New York, where Tomie went to art school

Time Line

1934
born

1952
goes to
art school

Tomie went to the
Museum of Modern Art
whenever he could.
He looked at the paintings
to learn more about art.

Museum of Modern Art, New York. Visitors look at
art by Ben Shahn, a famous artist whom Tomie liked.

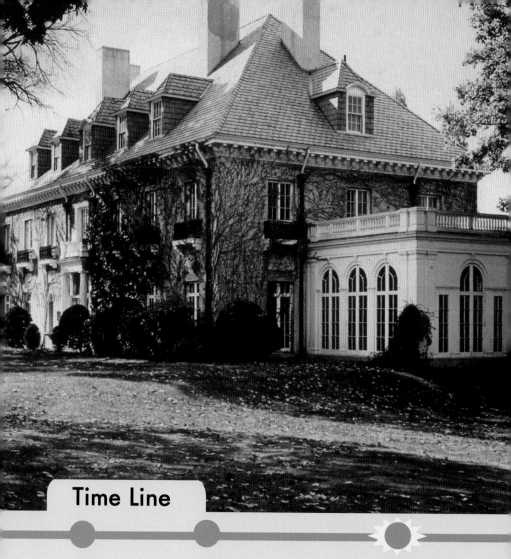

Time Line

| 1934 born | 1952 goes to art school | 1962 becomes an art teacher |

First Jobs

Tomie became an
art teacher after college.
In 1965, he drew pictures
for a science book.
It was his first job
as a book illustrator.

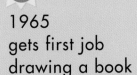 Newton College in Massachusetts, where Tomie
worked as an art teacher

1965
gets first job
drawing a book

Time Line

1934
born

1952
goes to
art school

1962
becomes an
art teacher

Tomie's Books

The first book Tomie
wrote and illustrated
was *The Wonderful
Dragon of Timlin.*
He made more books
in the next few years.

◀ Tomie painting a picture in his studio

1965
gets first job
drawing a book

1966
first book is
published

Time Line

1934
born

1952
goes to
art school

1962
becomes an
art teacher

Tomie made a book called *Nana Upstairs & Nana Downstairs*. Children enjoy this book about Tomie's grandmothers.

1965
gets first job
drawing a book

1966
first book is
published

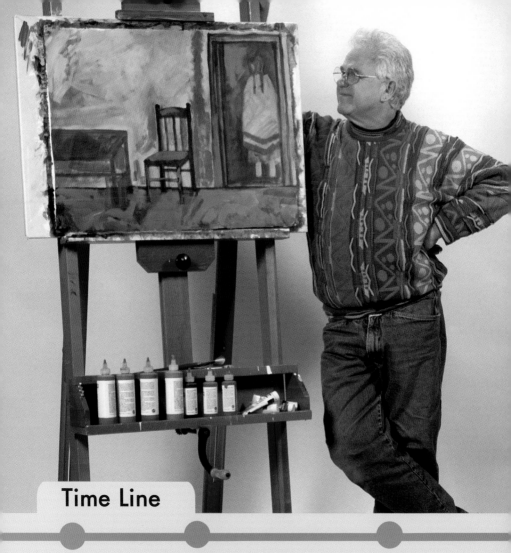

Time Line

1934	1952	1962
born	goes to	becomes an
	art school	art teacher

Tomie kept teaching art.
He kept writing
and illustrating books.
Kids love his books.
Adults do, too.

1965
gets first job
drawing a book

1966
first book is
published

Time Line

1934
born

1952
goes to
art school

1962
becomes an
art teacher

Tomie makes fun books. *Bonjour, Mr. Satie* is about a traveling cat. *Strega Nona* is about an old woman and a magic pot.

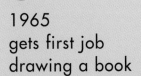 Tomie with a large picture from *Bonjour, Mr. Satie*

1965
gets first job
drawing a book

1966
first book is
published

1991
Bonjour, Mr. Satie
is published

Time Line

1934
born

1952
goes to
art school

1962
becomes an
art teacher

Tomie has illustrated
more than 200 books.
He has won many awards.
Tomie plans to
keep making books
for a long time.

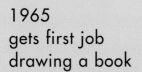

1965
gets first job
drawing a book

1966
first book is
published

1991
Bonjour, Mr. Satie
is published

Glossary

art—something beautiful that is made by drawing, painting, or crafting by hand

college—a school students go to after high school

graduate—to finish all required classes at a school

illustrate—to draw pictures for a book or other publication; people who draw pictures for books are called illustrators.

Read More

dePaola, Tomie. *Four Friends in Autumn.* New York: Simon & Schuster Books for Young Readers, 2004.

dePaola, Tomie. *Stagestruck.* New York: G. P. Putnam's Sons, 2005.

Woods, Mae. *Tomie dePaola.* Children's Authors. Edina, Minn.: Abdo, 2000.

Internet Sites

FactHound offers a safe, fun way to find Internet sites related to this book. All of the sites on FactHound have been researched by our staff.

Here's how:

1. Visit *www.facthound.com*
2. Type in this special code **0736836411** for age-appropriate sites. Or enter a search word related to this book for a more general search.
3. Click on the **Fetch It** button.

FactHound will fetch the best sites for you!

Index

art school, 7
art teacher, 11, 17
awards, 21
books, 11, 13, 15,
   17, 19, 21
born, 5
college, 11
Connecticut, 5

draw, 5, 7, 11
family, 5, 15
graduated, 7
high school, 7
illustrate, 11, 13, 17, 21
Museum of Modern Art, 9
New York, 7
write, 5, 13, 17

Word Count: 196
Grade: 1
Early-Intervention Level: 16

Editorial Credits
Mari C. Schuh, editor; Heather Kindseth, set designer; Patrick D. Dentinger,
   book designer; Kelly Garvin, photo researcher; Scott Thoms, photo editor

Photo Credits
Capstone Press/Karon Dubke, 14
Corbis/Schenectady Museum; Hall of Electrical History Foundation, 4
Courtesy of Pratt Institute, 6
Getty Images Inc./Hulton Archive, 8
Globe Photos/Adam Scull, 18
John J. Burns Library, Boston College, 10
2004 Suki Coughlin Photography/Paula McFarland Stylist, cover, 1, 12, 16, 20